SOME THINGS MATTER: 63 SONNETS

James Nash is a writer and poet, and a long-term resident of Leeds. He is a well known provider of creative writing workshops in schools, universities and in the community, and is regularly called on as a host of literary events.

Some Things Matter: 63 Sonnets is the fourth collection of his poetry. Highlights from the three previous collections, along with some new non-sonnet material, were published by Valley Press as an ebook in April 2012, under the title *A Bit of an Ice Breaker: Selected and Uncollected Poems*.

SOME THINGS MATTER

63 Sonnets

JAMES NASH

VP

Valley Press

First published in 2012 by Valley Press
Woodend, The Crescent, Scarborough, YO11 2PW
www.valleypressuk.com

Second edition, first printing (October 2014)

ISBN 978-1-908853-04-2
Cat. no. VP0038

A CIP record for this book is available from the British Library.

Printed and bound in Great Britain by
TJ International Ltd, Padstow, Cornwall

www.valleypressuk.com/authors/jamesnash

To Patricia for forty-three years of friendship,
and David for eight years of great happiness

Thanks go to my writer friends Anna Turner, Rachel Connor, Tom Palmer and Milly Johnson for their tremendous support during the writing of this collection, to poet David Tait for inspiring me to write in the sonnet form in the first place, to Felix Hodcroft for his wonderful input, and to Jason Edwards for his generous and careful reading of these sonnets at different stages in their development.

Sonnet 33 first appeared in *Here Come the Girls* by Milly Johnson.

SOME
THINGS
MATTER

63 SONNETS

2012

1.

If you should ever go, my heart would break,
Leaving a house of empty rooms behind.
If you should go, be careful what you take,
Some things matter, but others I'd not mind.
So take the books, the CDs and the fridge,
The pictures from the wall, the bathroom sink,
Take the front garden, and the laurel hedge,
For these are not important things, I think.
But leave your imprint upon the pillow,
And the faded tee-shirt you wear in bed,
Leave the battered sofa, and its hollow,
On the arm, where you always rest your head.
For if you should go, there is no doubt,
In truth, it's you I could not do without.

2.

Early morning, as I make my escape
Towel-wrapped from the bathroom shower,
Stopping briefly when I see the shape
Of my wet foot-prints on the floor.
My toes, the soles and heels of my two feet,
Like something from a children's story book,
With perfection in the silhouette,
As if an autograph, my own true mark.
When I return I find that they have nearly gone,
Dried up and leaving just a watery tear,
To vanish later in the morning sun;
And I wonder what I'll leave behind me here,
How light the traces I have made since birth,
Evaporating on the sun-baked earth.

3.

I used to wander through the bluebell woods,
Alone and free, told no-one where I went,
Wild with spring-time and the exploding buds,
And half-drunk on the flowers' bruised blue scent.
But those days are gone. Now I spend my time,
Gently patrolling the allotment's rows.
Where once grew wild garlic, metre and rhyme
Now lead my heart away from prose.
My patch is there amongst the other plots,
Where I prune and trim in daylight hours,
Foster tender plants in greenhouse pots,
And grow alternate rows of herbs and flowers.
Though twelve lines and a couplet may seem tame,
Words still thrust through and bloom, I find, the same.

4.

By chance I found a green and private place,
Which I had never visited before,
After the heat and roar it felt like grace,
The grassy stones, the church, its open door
To a hall of windows, their colours bright,
The pews and high beams of black carved wood,
Walls and ceilings gleaming a simple white,
The sun through the glass stained my skin like blood.
Inside only muted sounds could be heard,
The city's heart and pulse a distant thrum,
The high, trilling call of a single bird
Piercing the traffic boom of bass and drum.
And I heard through all this, as if a dream,
A small, clear voice that spoke aloud my name.

5.

It took forty years to really hear that song,
Not her greatest, for it to break my heart,
And I wonder why it took that long
To feel the sharp pertinence of her art.
Was it a chance and perfect combination,
Car radio and winter sea, that sprung
This sadness on me, that my generation,
Stardust and golden, were no longer young?
And we'd had so much hope that it seemed
The world was full of love enough to bend,
We listened to those songs, believed and dreamed,
That things might change, that want and war might end.
So tread past him softly, that man of middle years
Whose lost ideals have blurred his face with tears.

6.

The rain is silent, it has breathed a hush
In street and lamp-lit haven where I sit.
When he appears in a glistening rush,
More a water god, than domestic cat,
I ignore him, in my desire to read,
As round me he begins to hoop and beg,
So strongly insistent that I pay heed,
Rubbing his wet fur against my bare leg.
Most cats run on heat and solar power,
They charge up each day by fireside, in sun,
Mine is hydro-electric, one shower
Gives him at least an hour or two to run.
So he shakes himself with a joyful cry,
Fur crackles, as sparks of water fly.

7.

An ex-superhero comes to my gym.
Working away in a tattered old vest,
I try not to stare openly at him,
That big, faded letter on his old chest,
At those knee-length boots, and the square, square jaw,
Sixty-five years old if he's a day;
It's the brown leather belt you can't ignore,
And the baggy trunks which give him away.
I wonder what made him give up the task
Of righting wrongs, and saving mankind,
But I'm too polite to come out and ask,
As it's clear his powers are long behind.
He arrives on the bus, using his pass,
A regular to my Pilates class.

8.

Some say they don't like the sculptures here,
The curves which reflect each Yorkshire hill,
As if their wings like knives might score the sky,
Their metal and stone could crush and kill.
My sense is different; I walk in sun and rain
And find enduring themes to touch and hold,
Sometimes it's how the passing clouds can stain,
The bronze to dark, the sun turn it to gold,
The complexities of our human soul,
Wrought and chiseled, brought here and scattered then,
As beads from a necklace might break and roll,
We piece them together as best we can.
I feel my spirit grow and begin to sing,
I see, fresh-eyed, the tragedies of spring.

9.

A silver heart hangs from a Spanish chain,
Rosary of hope in the coming years,
There when I wake next in the dark again,
My spirit shrinking at the night-time fears.
It feels more durable than flesh and blood,
For human hearts can stop at any time,
And bodies go too quick to chalk and mud,
And who can guess the life-span of a rhyme?
Whoever will find it, and when and how,
Discovering it black with tarnish then,
May be much too far away to know
The names and histories of we two men,
Only that someone loved enough to part
With the Spanish chain and the silver heart.

10.

I have no offspring, and now never will
See parts of me get up and walk around,
A needle-thrust that can surprise me still,
But not the wilderness I thought I'd find,
With many things which shine this present bright,
Reflect my life to me, and give me heart
In this darkened theatre where we recite,
And cannot see how short or long our part.
So I count them, those things that always lift
My spirits – friends, sun in the garden now,
This recent verse, an unexpected gift
Which shows my heart the way, my spirit how.
Though these new seeds have only just been sown,
I live in hope to see my children grown.

11.

Of garden flowers I love honesty,
Which was woven throughout my garden once,
Self-seeding to grow where it chose to be,
Informal amongst more suburban plants.
I loved this buccaneering randomness
And the puritan contrast of its name,
And why it vanished I could never guess,
Though my garden did not after feel the same.
I wondered why it was no longer there,
And for a friend I mourned the empty space,
Then today I found a dark red flower,
Honesty had returned to take its place.
I will watch it until white seed-heads come,
Collect each black pearl, and then scatter them.

12.

I am constructing a new religion
From the part we've played in each other's life,
And this is not a sudden decision,
I've had years to shape and form belief,
Forty years of growing from boy to man,
From not admitting that all things must end,
To recognising how brief our span,
As I hurtle around the final bend.
There will be no church, we are free of rules
Which cheerlessly masquerade as God's will,
Just loyalty and caring which never cools,
And which sustain my friendship for you still.
Proof of my belief is in our story,
This my new god. Glory. Glory. Glory.

13.

It's not the midnight battering on the door,
The breaking in, and the violent arrest,
Nor any present persecution, that I fear,
But there is a terror I've not expressed.
I cannot claim to have ever suffered
From being with you, in any way at all,
[And so much love was freely offered
Us at our partnership in Leeds Town Hall],
My paranoia, perhaps habitual,
Of a future where they might hate our kind,
Is, that taking part in a public ritual,
We've made ourselves far easier to find.
Our names, our addresses, for all to read,
They might still hunt us down, and make us bleed.

14.

I still sense him everywhere I go,
Shadow moving behind me silently,
Sombre elegance slipping to and fro,
But vanished when I turn to check and see.
In addition to this gentle haunting,
From him whose love I had for just a year.
I see him in a Georgian painting
Prancing, ready to test the heath-land air.
Or in an ancient fresco on a wall
Of mounted warriors with sideways glances,
Whose bows and spears are bristling tall
Amongst the horses' hooves he dances.
Caspar's noble spirit is with us yet,
We shall remember him. We shall not forget.

15.

See them bursting from the kitchen cupboard,
A growing disaster that creaks and sags,
Stuffed in so tightly from port to starboard
My pesky collection of eco-bags.
The virtuous glow of doing right
By the planet, has been quite cancelled out,
Now it's less a choice and much more a fight
To pull one from a hundred just as stout.
Oh 'bags for life', I can't really deny,
I'd need twenty lives to use them all up,
So what will happen to them when I die,
A crappy legacy, a poisoned cup,
For my niece's children, and their children.
Perhaps just hope for reincarnation.

16.

The sun hangs low over the ruined church
Glazing the river with the gleam of ice,
While in the trees three ravens perch,
Hunched in their wings, guardians of this place.
Trains used to stop here, but now no more,
We just slow at curve and climb of line,
And I add these images to my store,
Of happiness, against some future time.
Let us rejoice in the sacrificial sky
As distant clouds and hills go up in flame,
The last days of the year shiver and die,
Sentries for whom we have no rank or name.
From the ashes of their funeral pyre,
Is born the clamour of another year.

17.

Your skin is cool and soft and smells of you,
When I wake to the pricking of night fear.
You sleep, and are quite oblivious to,
The rocks and shoals through which I steer.
We're on different journeys through this night,
I am awake and you sail far away,
Though your body is close and I hold it tight,
You may not stir until the birdsong day.
'Til then I have your breath to listen to,
Can inhale your sweet and precious scent,
And warmed by being so close to you,
May sleep again, with all my terrors spent.
We float on this raft together, we touch,
And on this long voyage take turns on watch.

18.

These were the clothes that once took my shape
That creased as I do at elbow and knee,
That covered me from ankle to my nape,
Were frayed and worn in places just like me.
These were the clothes in wardrobe and in drawer
That coloured my life in flowers and checks,
Sometimes strewn, a crime-scene, on bedroom floor,
Their limbs outflung as if in death or sex.
And now they're gathered up in plastic bags,
Piled up ready to be taken elsewhere,
A sleeve trails out, as if it sadly lags,
Grazing me with an unexpected fear.
What if when these garments are gone at last,
I mourn those faded textures of my past?

19.

I stand in the morning garden and weep,
The scent of jasmine in the warming air,
As if I've woken from an enchanted sleep,
Flooded by memories of when and where.
They took me to a long forgotten place,
Living again what I lived as a boy,
Though the window reflects another's face,
I am caught by the perfume of past joy.
We breathe in this past when we breathe in scent,
Shrug on youthful clothes, and cry youthful tears,
As if the time between has not been spent
On the business of living all those years.
The jasmine blooms, it is not finished yet.
Its scent is strong. Do you remember it?

20.

My lungs are slack bellows, I have no breath,
Sleep squeezed my throat shut, and will not return,
I sit on the bath, contemplate my death,
Is this a rehearsal or am I done,
Trapped in the 'en-suite' of my hotel room,
Eyes screwed and bloodshot, at this final test?
I have no choice of when or what might come,
And curse the useless organ in my chest.
If I could pray, I would pray for relief,
Not to be saved, just for courage enough
In these last few moments, however brief,
To offer some thanks with each choking cough.
But night drains away greyly, through a sieve,
Letting dawn seep in; it seems I may live.

21.

I have been here before, decades ago,
And was still a boy when I first explored
These lanes and villages. My pace was slow
As time was something I could well afford.
Nothing much has changed in what I see,
I recognise the fields and woods and moor,
Except what I look on now is never free
From meaning I'm not even searching for.
So branches meet overhead and then link
Like translucent fingers across the lane,
We travel in green light, sometimes we sink
Into shadow, sometimes we rise again.
Yet the dark will come and seasons turn,
Rehearsals from which there is much to learn.

22.

I love this dark, each granite twist and turn,
Long since gave up meadows for this maze,
And if at times for company I yearn,
There are those poor, lost ones on whom I graze.
I do not miss the sun, the burnished air,
My knotted heart cannot conceive of love,
I have taught myself to be happy here,
Not pine for, or miss, the world above.
But sometimes as I wander through these halls,
A green breath of spring can seep below,
I shrink, my horns scrape useless on these walls,
Against my will let out a muted low,
Then snort and bellow, toss my bullish head,
I hate such signs of hope. I wish them dead.

23.

When the last drunken shouts had died away,
And I became aware of muted light,
My hotel room slowly suffused with grey,
Pre-dawn snuffling at the heels of night,
With care I drew the curtains so as not to wake
Him, who shares my journey for this little while,
The sea was still and calm, almost a lake,
Tiny rills curling round the bay a mile.
And morning filled my heart with leaping joy,
The sea, the sky, the sun. Just everything.
And I was once again that dreaming boy.
Who, of every landscape, was almost king.
How hard then to turn and reflected see,
My older, present self. No majesty.

24.

I love these days which seem to last so long,
When we can sit out in the garden late,
Listening to the hidden blackbird's song,
Under the beech in green and noble state,
Not long before the chilly wind arrives,
And reminds us which things are done for good,
How love is blown and scattered like the leaves,
And the beech is cut and sawn for fire-wood.
Past memories must be hoarded still
Against the darkness and against the loss,
They will warm us, so we must distil
The spirit of these days of happiness.
It will help the other to carry on
As darkness falls, and one of us has gone.

25.

And if there are no stories left to tell,
No grand summings-up, no recording of the past,
If those ships have gone beyond the swell,
With no lingering sight of sail or mast
And if I am marooned here quite alone,
Until my voice begins to rust and fade,
My flesh deserting each and every bone,
What monument, if any, will I have made?
Perhaps just a bundle of what I feel
Tied together tightly, my heart, my core,
For the sun will shine, hot, implacable,
The seas will ebb and flow forever more.
Some give their names to stars in vain to prove
They were. I do not need to. I've known love.

26.

I see my age written in the other's face,
We have the same furrow in our forehead here,
I see the lines my mother had, the lace
Whose pattern deepened with each passing year.
I see the brackets of my father's frown
And frailty in the quiver of his hand,
The body slowly beginning to let him down,
The brown marks on skin like grains of sand.
I look closer and see traces everywhere,
Of a tottering empire, crumbling slow,
This was a domain of which he took such care,
And this was his palace, now brought so low.
The mirror lends back my own face to me,
I find secrets there I'd not thought to see.

27.

They come overnight, like invading troops,
Camp out on the lawn in the morning sun,
By midday they idly sit round in groups,
As if the battle is already won.
I attack them with a serial-killer spleen,
Unsure of the origin of this hate,
It's not as if my lawn's a bowling green,
And other intruders don't meet this fate.
I mow their golden heads off, put to death
The over-exuberance of early May,
Wild garlic falls bleeding with onion breath,
While honeyed euphorbia scents the day.
They'll get revenge if they have the chance,
But not, I'm hoping, with incontinence.

28.

Your friendship was always a poisoned cup
Of malice posing as sparkling wit,
Which when lifted to the lips to sup,
I found green-eyed envy had sugared it.
The world to you was a hideous joint
Whose workings puzzled you, filled you with hate,
And you'd missed somehow the obvious point
That friends are not there to manipulate.
So what can I wish you in your world of pain,
To drag you out of your deep, deep pit,
What is missing that you need to regain,
Which will enable you to conquer it?
I wish you contentment, friends to stroke you.
I wish you love. Although it may choke you.

29.

Homewards. Overground on the underground,
Fields and house-scapes I simply don't recall.
Getting off, I walk through streets until I find
My birthplace, and I wonder what I'll feel.
My home until eighteen, and then no more,
Where one tree made the road an avenue.
No memories left here worth coming for,
Or insights I might bring back north to you.
I stand here and I feel little. Nothing.
There's no connection left, to signify,
With this house, this suburban coffin,
A monument to sixties D.I.Y.
Although I'm staring like an obsessed lover,
I can only see what dad fucked over.

30.

You said that you needed a much bigger sky,
And I put it down to your fenland past,
That horizons in cities made you sigh.
[I heard a whisper then, that this won't last].
I, who come from a more suburban root,
Quite liked the interplay of roofs and trees,
But knew not all things would the other suit,
In partnership; we'd need to compromise.
It's only now I have divined your meaning,
The truth was hidden from me, or I had hid
Below the surface, so unruffled seeming,
A deeper sense of what you meant and said.
Looking back it's clear I was the one,
Shrinking your sky, and blotting out your sun.

31.

The dead wasp lies on the window sill
Striped and articulated myrmidon.
And empty of its buzzing, clockwork will,
A hollow case, all angry life has gone.
It stung; I admit to being quite unmanned,
Retaliating with a book of verse,
The Four Quartets first came to hand,
My finger's sore, I know the wasp feels worse.
I put aside remaining childish fright,
And creep to where the murder victim fell,
No gentle exit into that good night,
It is already in time past, a shell.
If this is Death, this rugby-shirted thing,
I fear thee still; I know whereof thy sting!

32.

What is he thinking, the old man who mows,
Cutting a swathe through the hot afternoon,
Beheading the buttercups as he goes,
A brief storm of gold, that's over too soon?
He is tuning his words to make you a song
To sing through the cough of the mower's blade,
His message is simple, meaning is long,
Blessing this day when promises are made.
His task is wearisome, he wishes it done,
So on he toils in the last of the light,
To flame in the eye of the setting sun,
And then fall as dew in the shiv'ry night.
He's left these green spaces clear for you now,
Rest here a short while, and let your love grow.

33.

On the third day out I get it, the sea
Is not one thing, it constantly transforms
Itself, in an unthinking majesty
Tapestries horizons with sun or storms.
And then lying here, rocking to and fro
On its soothing and gentle amniotic swell,
I loosen thoughts of home, and let them go,
So my shipwrecked heart can start to heal.
What promise for me, what spirit salve,
When unanchored here I find at last,
Something has shifted, giving me resolve
To let hope aboard, jettison the past.
The sea has granted me a chance to live,
Led us maybe to a safe harbour, love.

34.

Through the open window I taste the air
Of chilled morning. I see the golden light
Touch the garden, like an answered prayer,
After the sulky darkness of the night.
The year is turning, summer nearly done,
The fennel's yellow crown bowed by the rain
In the lost kingdom of a watery sun,
While lavender breathes its last scent in vain.
There are no ways to halt the year's decay,
Before it moulders and its heat is lost,
Like roses which gamble afresh each day,
Until at last they brown and crack with frost.
In this autumn, it's harder to ignore
How Nature drenches us in metaphor.

35.

Today I found some clover in my lawn:
How bucolic is my inner-city,
[I'd thought the boundaries more strictly drawn]
I mowed around them, they were so pretty.
'Rus in urbe', some ancient Roman said,
And that is what I have exactly here,
The first thing I see when I creak from bed,
For that early, elderly, post-pee peer.
Others would dig them out and shout and curse,
Call them interlopers, and weep and wail,
Yelling out their hatred, and much, much worse,
Like mindless headlines in the Daily Mail.
Here all flowers will be allowed to grow,
The grass may sigh, but shares its portion now.

36.

I will mourn you now before you leave,
So I do not weep on that farewell day,
Can just hold you back by your scarf or sleeve,
And say in truth you only brought me joy.
So if my cheeks aren't uniformed by loss,
And any signs of grief are close to nought
You know it's not that I don't give a toss,
These were battles that I've already fought.
So I will grieve you now, and not too late,
And there are many tears for me to shed,
If I'm to smile at the departure gate,
All sadness gone, because I'd thought ahead.
But such strategies won't be proof, I fear,
Against the sudden storming of a tear.

37.

Talk to the woman who walks in the woods,
Who greets all the seasons as her friend,
Tramping the paths and the fields with her dogs,
Where past and present and future blend.
Walking where she walked five decades ago,
Where the kingfisher darts, vivid blue flame.
Her life in this valley, sunshine and snow,
Is engraved on her face, by wind and by rain.
People and places share geology,
In each line on the face, groove of the beck
The wearing of time is clear to see.
We walk through the woods, with no turning back,
Our lives as fleeting, but somehow as true,
As the kingfisher's sudden flash of blue.

38.

I was given them twenty years ago,
Two pink camellias for my garden,
Forty, there didn't seem much time to go
To finally make my fame and fortune.
I planted them with much thought and care
So I could see them when I came home
On either side of my then front door,
Two glossy-leaved shrubs exactly the same.
And when I moved here, my self uprooted,
I brought one with me to plant again.
From sun to deepest shade, it seemed fated,
To have fewer blossoms and lose its shine.
But the surprise, after a score of years,
Is how this April, my God, the flowers!

39.

I want to be bathed in warm asses' milk,
I want to be fed Maltesers all day long,
I want a boudoir for me to sit and sulk,
I want to be spoiled – how can that be wrong?
Instead I spend all day in the cliché mines,
Scrabbling for diamonds, or at the least, quartz,
Where I rub at dull stones to make them shine,
Smuggling them out in my underpants.
Long shifts in this literary abattoir,
Up to my elbows in a sonnet's guts,
Poetry piecework for hour after hour,
Making something new from verbal off-cuts.
For that's the challenge, not poems like this,
Which, if truth be told, are a piece of piss.

40.

Last night he arrived with mysterious force
Into my garden, woke me with a sigh,
Breathed to me as he rustled through the grass,
Though his breath was honey, the year must die.
He coughed and whirled the summer parasol,
Stirring up leaves as he cleared his throat,
And from a night corner he seemed to fill
The dark with elegies of horn and flute.
He whispered to me of times long gone,
As I dozed and dreamed in my linen lair,
That I must lose all I depend upon,
Get used again to this chill in the air.
We met as brothers who had been estranged,
I am grown older, but he has not changed.

41.

There's a beech tree nearby I feel is mine
Though sovereign in its pomp and power;
Some trees have magnificence, they are fine
Palaces of dream, whose seasons inspire.
We are not such trees which fill all with awe,
We have different grace, a slighter mode,
A sparse copse of silver birch, blown and raw,
Half-anonymous by an urban road.
But through successive years we are as one,
Our moonstruck trunks are neighbours, leaves entwine,
We share the winter winds, the summer sun,
And our roots grow deep as our hearts combine.
Thank you then, for what you have given free
In your faithful sojourn here, next to me.

42.

Were you there always, hiding in the wood,
Waiting for me to gouge and scrape you out,
Just sleeping in the grain, my little bud,
So deep beneath a timber coverlet?
You emerge, still and solemn, in the light,
Of this new day, and wonder who you are,
Damp with the resin of your wooden night.
My tools are sharp, and you have travelled far
Since, a miracle of nature, you grew
Along with others and gave me shade,
'Till felled and quartered, I took hold of you,
And from your ending something fresh was made.
I may have done nothing with my small art,
But conjure some life to your kindling heart.

43.

The train creeps across Yorkshire into moors,
Small mountains where stone cottages have grown
And spread along the ridge and valley floors
Like rock outcroppings amongst the green.
I sit there watching mills and chimneys pass,
The towns and villages long built on wool,
High summer, and I see how green the grass
Is before it browns, and how the trees are full.
The promise is at its highest and yet,
This holds the seeds of death and decay,
I search my heart and find no regret
As outside the sun glitters on the day.
Sixty-three summers I've seen come and go,
This mimic birth and death is what I know.

44.

With the snowfall came a different light,
Subverting the darkness, so that it shone,
Muffling too the ragged traffic of the night,
As if the street were hushed and drowned in moon.
Fearful and haunted by my shadow past,
I was drowsy, half-woken from my sleep,
Still wary in case those dreams should last,
Hunched in vigil, as snow piled bright and deep.
But with each flake my heart began to warm,
This false dawn, with no motive to deceive,
Had brought with its beauty, peace and calm
From night horrors, a welcome reprieve.
Outside the day begins with filtered sun,
I am myself. The conquered night is done.

45.

If you need a monument, just look round
To see what I saw, to stroll where I strolled;
You might find things of beauty where I found
Them; I seek no permanence in the world.
Only perhaps sometimes, in some people's hearts,
To be recalled, as the briefest quickening
In their veins, felt as a season departs,
As winter's grip unlocks and lets in spring.
No cathedral to stand in stone for me,
No statue or brass plaque to put on show,
Perhaps an occasional memory,
Of something I was wont to say or do.
Or a passing remark that I was kind,
If that's my memorial, I'll not mind.

46.

The woman on the bus is old and deaf
Sharing her story with a tutting friend
And us, the frozen parties to her grief
For brother, husband, son; it's not defined.
He phones her still almost every night,
But doesn't talk, she hears just storm and wind,
Then gropes out sideways to switch on the light,
And trembling, tries to right her capsized mind.
But her heart, she thinks, will never mend,
Will never believe that it's really true,
If only she'd been there to grasp his hand,
In that breath-stolen second when he knew.
She quietens as her destination nears,
Her eyes a foreign sea of unshed tears.

47.

Tree roots wind tight through our ribs and spine,
Their tendrils clutch us hard and strong,
While above the ground there is not one sign,
Our voice so weak, you might not hear this song.
Sometimes a creature stirs within our skull,
And we are reminded of what we would not know
The sudden bullet-cracks, and then how full
The pit we had dug in the tousled snow,
Dying screams cut short, and when no-one came,
Companions in death, then tangled bone.
It has been so long, no-one knows our name,
As if all trace or dust of us has flown.
Remember us in what you do or say,
We who sleep nameless beneath this tree.

48.

I unfold the map, and then smooth it out,
So that the entire city can be seen,
Paper-folds cross many a path and route,
Confusing many places where I've been.
I've travelled all round on bike and bus,
Craning my neck to see where roads might go,
Often travelling to the terminus,
With no other motive than just 'to know'.
How would it be if my whole life were mapped,
Showing sunlit road and abandoned track,
The times I was happy, times I felt trapped,
With no way out of some dark cul-de-sac?
How hard it would be to open that chart,
Retrace the journeys which led to this heart.

49.

Men are quite dangerously erotic,
Only look at them if you really must,
One fleeting glimpse might be so hypnotic
You'd not be able to control your lust.
Oh cover the men, protect us from them,
That hint of ankle, that turn of their necks
And their lustrous hair which can strike us dumb,
Everything about them just reeks of sex.
I'm considering entire body garments,
From head to toe, for the whole of their life,
This will ensure that the only moments
That a man can be seen are by his wife.
And always cover their keys, to conceal,
That sudden penile flash of brass or steel.

50.

I look and make no sense of it at all,
The shards of smashed-up glasses on the floor,
What happened to make the cabinet fall,
Was it a nudging cat, or slamming door?
I wail in horror at the loss and shock,
The junk-shop finds, each loving gift,
Pick out the few preserved by luck,
And through the jewelled rubble sift.
Oh, the sharpness of past times mixed
And broken in a crunching heap.
Destroyed and gone are things I thought were fixed,
Now jagged memories for me to keep.
Broken glass has more power than it should
To glitter in my hands while it draws blood.

51.

When I bought my first bunch of flowers
From her little shop with the name above,
I was still so young and so light in years,
I had no names yet for the blooms I'd love.
And then I saw her some weeks ago,
Saw how her skull was showing in her face,
Knew what had been in her and growing slow,
Was speeding up to a murderous pace.
I wondered what her memorial might be,
Who had lived her life among leaf and scent,
Where once blossoms were crammed for all to see,
Was now two empty rooms and up for rent.
Until this week, her window full once more
With flowers left by others at her door.

52.

We are easy to kill. This thing we know,
Bodies are fragile: it wouldn't take much
To smash his skull with a random blow,
The kiss of a boot, or a truncheon's touch.
There might be another story to tell
How he actually died. No-one confessed,
If he fought for breath on the floor of a cell,
With two of them sitting hard on his chest.
No-one remembers, for no-one was there,
A convenient amnesia has taken his place.
So we have to live without being sure,
Imagining his tears, the look on his face.
All life is sacred, but there's just one hitch,
We are easy to kill, off like a switch.

53.

I was born at home, as most of us were,
To my mother's screams in an upstairs room,
Arriving with no help of gas or air,
In that immediate post-war, baby-boom.
How did she love me? I can only guess
At her strength of feeling, holding me so
Tightly, with such care, fierce tenderness,
Unable to bear the letting me go.
Did I love her? This is complicated,
There were years I felt a simple dislike,
And loving her was something I hated,
Had to escape, perhaps even to break.
But Mother, for the first time since you died
I feel a liking for you kick inside.

54.

I met a woman once with violet eyes
Which had been her downfall. I looked in
Them then, saw the lost hopes, the tawdry lies
That men had told her, and the years of gin.
It had not been enough that special blue,
To bring her what she wanted, not at all.
If men really loved her she never knew,
Was it her eyes that caused each one to fall?
To be sure she was still pretty enough
At fifty-one, for many heads to turn,
A cut-price Cleopatra, who'd known it rough,
But could somehow make men want and yearn.
I saw violets today, growing by my front door,
So small, so shy, that blue. I thought of her.

55.

Sadly there is no Victoria Cross
For human gallantry in the everyday,
The acts of love, experience of loss,
The briars which block and snag our way.
If there were you'd be awarded one,
For exceptional courage under fire,
For surviving cold dawn and noonday sun,
The humdrum dramas which we each endure.
I'd strike a medal for being alive,
Just for those who do the best they can,
For when we're gone, what will survive
Are memories of the woman, and the man.
You'd pin it to your chest with ribboned pride,
To glimmer briefly on the dark'ning tide.

56.

I see a skein of geese across the sky,
Wings beating hard above the curving earth,
Look up and hear their distant, piping cry,
In this fortieth autumn since your birth.
I wonder at the instinct which drives them on,
Aware I should not make a human claim
For what they may feel as they fly as one.
It looks like love but with another name.
For on such journeys are miracles wrought
By those questing hearts, that share more than blood,
The wide world is conquered and storms are fought,
Leaving a few bright feathers in the mud.
And your own migrations result somehow
In this marvellous woman we love now.

57.

I sometimes feel I'd like to scrub my brain,
Of things I've witnessed which I can't be rid,
Excise all loss and horror scene by scene
Allow me to walk with a lighter tread.
The kicking to death in the high rise flats,
The prisoner's limbs quilted with self-harm,
The boy who told me how he tortured cats,
These lodge in my brain and can kidnap calm.
I am not asking for a world of nice,
Where nothing bad is allowed to be,
Beauty and kindness sometimes will suffice
To disarm these jabbings of memory.
But oh, to feel nothing and be no-one,
To have weekends off from being human.

58.

I asked a famous writer once what she
Wrote about. And she paused and took a breath,
Eschewing blandness she confounded me,
When her answer came as, 'sex and death'.
And yes, artists deal with mortality
And the consequences of love and sex,
But in this stage of life, I seem to see
Time in everything, and its effects.
My life-span is long enough to measure,
The growth of the great trees, and how they've spread
In the churchyard where I pause at leisure,
To muse on the now, not so recent dead.
While love still flowers around the stones,
I see only a camouflage for bones.

59.

Old soldier bleeds purple, hangs his thinning head,
His shanks laid bare with every passing breeze,
Surrendering all youth now that summer's fled,
His heavy booty loading autumn trees.
He was here in springtime when his blood flowed green
And it seemed there were no battles to be fought,
Carefree through summer fields he might be seen
Scattering poppies; all that's come to nought.
For now with a stripped hedgerow crutch he limps
Slow and painful down familiar ways,
Hoping for some trace perhaps, one last glimpse
Of that youthful self in these emb'ring days.
Old soldier bleeds purple, but is not afraid,
Squares his shoulders against the coming blade.

60.

An invisible wind gusts through our lives
Which we make visible, so you can see
Our pathways, as we are blown like leaves,
Spinning together for just a little way.
Sometimes in a storm we are torn apart,
To be piled in drifts, or by ivy held,
Exposing our veins and our tattered heart,
Before crumbling at last to earth and mould.
I have no wishes and no special pleas,
For the final journey that I must make;
Save warm sunshine in these autumn days,
That Night Wind grasps me before I wake.
Anything to escape the high-back chairs,
The smell of piss, while non-stop telly blares.

61.

There is no democracy. We are owned
By media moguls and off-shore banks;
Universal suffrage, it seems just loaned,
Lies beneath the treads of advancing tanks.
There is no democracy. I can't find
A trace, cut down and poisoned at its roots,
Where government has a single cast of mind,
Those egregious, smirking boys in suits.
So out of control are these selfish ones,
They would close anything that they don't use,
Attack the vulnerable, blame all their sins
On the hapless, helpless who cannot choose.
There is no democracy. Money rules,
Our rights eroded, we've been had for fools.

62.

And will there still be singing in the dawn
When wind frets and scythes through threadbare trees,
When ice has mirrored over path and lawn,
And the hymns of last summer gasp and freeze?
Yes, the fraying threads of a piping song
Will still be heard from branch and ivy wall,
From hearts so frail but still so fiercely strong,
Warm sparks that flicker with uneven call.
There will still be singing I promise you
A victory song after frozen night,
Though the tunes are held by those very few,
Who cling on until the warming light.
Can you hear them, in one courageous voice,
Sing of returning spring? They have no choice.

63.

Standing here, chilled by a wintry sea
Of different faiths, rattling on this beach,
Some whose utter certainties frighten me
Others' complexities float, just out of reach,
I try to find words for the essence, the bones
Of any faith to which I can cleave,
Against all the odds, and amidst these storms,
What is it that I actually can believe?
I believe in your warm hands, [and what else?]
The sweet, straw smell of my sleeping dog's fur
above his beating heart, your ticking pulse,
all cause the tides of hope and faith to stir.
I can say [please know this 'you' is various]
I believe in you, in me. And in us.

THREE
MORE
SONNETS

2013

*The following sonnets were written in 2013 as
a commission for York and Cardiff Universities'
Chronic Disorders of Consciousness Research Centre.
James performed two of them on BBC Radio 3,
October 11th 2014.*

1.

Both of us witnessed when wingless you flew,
Headfirst Icarus, and gone in a blink,
Me, in my bedroom, with homework to do
Mum washing dishes below in the sink.
Mending the roof, your descent was unplanned
Ending loud and clumsy in the back yard
With hammer and nails still clutched in your hand,
Somehow alive though the impact was hard.
Now time, the healer, has not healed our loss,
For you are still here, though in what guise
And quite how much, it would be hard to guess,
From the twitch and flicker of your eyes.
We dive-bombed too, in the years since you fell,
And we, like you, have not landed well.

2.

I'm a shadow of a shadow, no more
The one you knew than a cloud in the sky
Can claim permanence. I've travelled so far
(My migrations still mysterious to me)
From any known region, no maps to chart
My journey. I'm a leaf whose flesh is rot,
Woman suspended, whose warm beating heart
Beat on when all about me had forgot.
This shadow state has light but not enough,
It's OK, but has none of the fire
I once knew before, before the cuff
Of accident, brain blown, loss of power.
Others remark on how well I've done,
Shadow woman; the other one has gone.

3.

We are all survivors, we bear the scars,
Faint tattoos telling stories of our life.
Some may read them, and others might have ears
Tuned to subtleties of our joy and grief.
There may be gains as summer follows spring,
When autumn drops and winter hollows out,
But then the seasons do not always bring
What we expect. We may not hear the shout
Of the youthful year, be lost to wintry beauty,
If we have moved to different, deeper dreams,
Far from the reaches of love, or duty,
Beyond the range of any others' claims.
We are all survivors, but it may be
That we survive only in memory.